Paulo Mendes da Rocha

King House
Millan/Leme House

Residential Masterpieces 27
Paulo Mendes da Rocha
King House
Millan/Leme House

Text by José Paulo Gouvêa
Photographs and edited by Yoshio Futagawa
Art direction: Gan Hosoya

Printed and bound in Japan

ISBN 978-4-87140-560-7 C1352

Paulo Mendes da Rocha

King House

São Paulo, Brazil, 1972

Millan/Leme House

São Paulo, Brazil, 1970

Text by José Paulo Gouvêa

Photographed by Yoshio Futagawa

世界現代住宅全集27

パウロ・メンデス・ダ・ローシャ
キング邸
サンパウロ，ブラジル　1972
ミラン／レミ邸
サンパウロ，ブラジル　1970

文：ジョゼ・パウロ・ゴヴェア

撮影・編集：二川由夫

サンパウロ，1970年代初頭の二つの住宅——ジョゼ・パウロ・ゴヴェア
Two Houses in the early 1970's in São Paulo *by José Paulo Gouvêa*

パウロ・メンデス・ダ・ローシャが1970年代初頭に手掛けた「ミラン邸」と「キング邸」は，特にプログラムの構成に関する解へのアプローチにユニークな特徴を持つ住宅である。都市問題の解としての一戸建て住宅は実行不可能であるとのメッセージ性から導かれたこれらのプロジェクトには，ブルジョワ的生活様式を必ずしも否定することなく緊張感を生み出すという明確な意図が込められており，建築家が自らの政治理念を実現するべく独自の言語と空間性を開拓した実験場である。

この二つの住宅の設計に携わった当時40代前半だったパウロ・メンデス・ダ・ローシャはサンパウロ大学の建築学科から強制的に引き離され，他の同僚たちと同様に軍事独裁政権による抑圧に苦しんでいた。

全面的に打放しコンクリートで覆われるこの二つの住宅は，同時期の建築家らによって育まれた言語，美的表現としての構造の優位性を提起している。1960年代初めからメンデス・ダ・ローシャと組んできたブラジル日系二世の土木技師シグエル・ミツタニと協同して設計された。

「ミラン／レミ邸」*
1970年建築の「ミラン邸」はサンパウロ西部の住宅街にある緑生い茂る小さな公園の向かいに位置し，地面を掘り下げ土に埋まるように建てられているのが特徴である。敷地の狭さと不規則な地形ゆえ，擁壁を家の内部に取り込むことで内部に特化した空間性をつくり上げることとなった。居間と台所のある1階部分は擁壁に

囲まれており，その上に寝室群を収める標準的なヴォリュームの梁構造が載せられる。寝室階のスラブの間にある開口部がつくる中央の吹抜けはトップライトに照らされている。この構造のおかげで住宅内には柱が無く，また外部に面した窓も無い。

ドローイングに見られる当初の設計では，住宅の内部空間と外の通りの都市空間との間の緊張感が明らかに意図されている。公道に敷かれたアスファルトがそのまま屋外パティオから家の中へと続き，居間と台所の床までを覆う。街路とパティオの間を物理的に隔てるものが何も無いことで，この内部空間は都市空間とひと続きになった敷地内への屋内アクセス路となる。通常は街路に使われるアスファルトの内部空間への流用は，この部分のプログラムの屋内的性質を覆す。

波打つ壁面がパティオと内部空間を隔てる。居間がおかれる中央の2層吹抜けは，建物の上部スラブに穿たれたトップライトを通り抜けることで弱められた外からの光と音に満たされた暗く静かな空間。天井からの光が中央の吹抜けを照らし，居間のアスファルト床と対象的な白いエポキシ材の床と打放しコンクリートによる螺旋階段を浮かび上がらせる。

居間と台所はコンクリート製のつくり付け家具により仕切られる。トップライトからの採光，換気を利用するよう設計された2層吹抜けの台所は寝室階のスラブと敷地側面の擁壁との空隙を埋めるかたちになっている。

よく工場などで使用される白いエポキシ樹脂のフローリングが寝室群を収めた

Designed by Paulo Mendes da Rocha in the early 1970s, Millan and King houses have a unique feature, specially in the way the issues related to the organization of the program are solved. From the statement of the unfeasibility of the single-family residence as a solution for urban problems, the projects clearly intend to create tension in the bourgeois way of life not necessarily denying it. The houses are the laboratory for the architect's political beliefs, developing a language and a spatiality of his own.

At the time the houses were designed, Paulo Mendes da Rocha, then in his early forties, was compulsorily away from the Architecture School of the University of São Paulo and suffered, along with other colleagues, the consequences of the repression implied by the military dictatorship.

Built entirely in exposed concrete, the houses present the predominance of the structure as an aesthetic expression, language that was also being developed in that period by other architects. The houses were designed in partnership with Siguer Mitsutani, a Brazilian civil engineer, son of Japanese immigrants who, since the early 1960s, had been working with Mendes da Rocha.

Millan/Leme House*
Built in 1970, the Millan house is located in a residential neighborhood in the western area of São Paulo, in front of a small park with dense vegetation. The singularity of this house is that it is embedded in the ground, as a result of an excavation. The small dimensions of the lot and the irregular topography determined this action by integrating the retaining walls into the house, creating a spati-

ality in which the main characteristic is to be exclusively internal. The retaining walls create the lower floor of the house, where the living room and the kitchen are located. Supported on these retaining walls, a regular volume structured by beans shelters the dormitories. An opening between the slabs of the dormitories creates a central void illuminated by a skylight. This structural solution allows the house to have no pillars or windows facing the exterior.

The original solution of the house, as seen in the drawings, clearly creates tension between the interior space of the residence and the outer and urban space of the street. The same asphalt that paves the public way enters the house by the external patio and also covers the floor of the living room and kitchen. The absence of any physical separation between the street and the patio makes this space a continuity of the urban space, an internal access road to the lot. Asphalt, a material traditionally used in the paving of streets, is also used as a lining of the inner space, subverting the domestic characteristics of these parts of the program.

A sinuous wall separates the patio from the internal space. The living room occupies the central void: a dark and silent double height ceiling space, where the external light and sound arrive muffled and filtered by the skylight installed in the upper slab of the building. The light coming from the ceiling illuminates the central void and highlights a circular staircase made of exposed concrete and white epoxy floor in contrast to the asphalt of the living room.

The living room and the kitchen are separated by concrete furniture. Illuminated and ventilated by skylight, the double height

上階全体を覆う。天井の高い子供用寝室は四つのセルに分けられ動線に沿って並べて配置されている。バスルームは共同，採光は台所に向けて開く窓から。低い天井の主寝室は中央の吹抜けに向けて大きく開かれ，居間と屋外パティオを隔てる壁によって仕切られている。この寝室階からはスタジオを抜けて金属製の螺旋階段から屋外パティオへとアクセスすることもできる。

　寝室間の動線は，ファサードの一部を構成するプールのある外部サンルームのヴォリュームへ延びている。プールの上の階段からは建物の屋根へ登ることができる。屋上は池のある庭園になっており，ここからは向かいの公園と町の一部の眺望が楽しめる。

　使用人の諸室は，住空間と都市空間のつながりや緊張感が及ばないような場所に配置されている。すなわち洗濯室と使用人用寝室は，屋外パティオから直接アクセスできる地下にあり，庭から採光を得る。

　2000年代初頭には新しい住人を迎えるにあたりパウロ・メンデス・ダ・ローシャ指揮の下リノベーションが行われ，建設当時の設計方針に大きな変更が加えられた。台所は住宅内部から，上階の床スラブ下，屋外パティオに置かれた白く塗られたコンクリートのヴォリューム内へと移設。歩道とパティオの境界線上に金属ゲートを設置。アスファルト床をセメント床に置き換え，また金属製螺旋階段の上部が撤去された。

「ジェームス・キング邸」
1972年に建てられた「キング邸」はサンパウロ南部のゲートに守られた居住地区にある。地区内にはこんもりとした森の中に様々な建築様式の大邸宅が点在し，それぞれの敷地は約2,000平方メートルと小規模な農場ほどの広さがある。

　その敷地の規模と周囲の環境ゆえ，この住宅はランドスケープ内において敷地の境界線がほとんど気づかれないような孤立したエレメントとして設計されることとなった。四角い平面を持つ1層の空間で，打放しコンクリートのヴォリュームが地下階から立ち上がる柱に支えられ浮いている。この高床式ヴォリュームには開口部が穿たれ，明るく開かれた中央パティオのまわりに居間，台所，洗濯室，ベランダといったこの家の共用エリアのすべてが配置される。寝室群はこのヴォリュームの陽の当たる側面に沿って，ブリーズ・ソレイユの背後に並べられている。家の中へはパティオ内の階段からアクセスする。

　敷地の自然な地形に合わせた地階は，広く独立した，開かれたフリースペースである。部分的に上を建物に覆われているためレジャーに供される空間には日当たりの良いエリアと日陰のエリアの両方がある。ここにはプールの他，地下に使用人用の寝室群がある。

　居間は，この住宅の中央部の広いスペースを占め，窓はパティオに開かれ，また背後の壁面は寝室へ通じる。各寝室は共用バスルームによって仕切られており，建物の陽の当たる側に沿って各寝室をつなぐ通路が住宅内のプライベート空間を

ceiling space designed for the kitchen occupies the void between the slab of the dormitories and the retaining wall in the side of the lot.

White epoxy flooring, commonly used in factories, coats the entire upper level of the house, where the bedrooms are. The children's bedrooms are four cells with tall ceiling heights arranged regularly in front of an access circulation, served by a shared bathroom and illuminated by internal windows that open towards the space of the kitchen. The master bedroom is a low ceiling space fully open to the central void and protected by the same wall that separates the living room and the outside patio. From this dormitory, through a small living room (studio), it is possible to access the external patio by a circular metal staircase.

Through the circulation of the rooms one access the external solarium where the pool is, a volume that composes the facade of the house. A stairway above the pool leads to the roof of the house, where there is a water garden from where is possible to view the park and part of the city.

The integration and friction between domestic space and urban space does not occur in the rooms occupied by the employees. Accessed directly from the external patio, the laundry and employees dormitories are situated in an underground level, illuminated by a garden.

In order to receive new residents, in the early 2000s, the house was renewed under the coordination of Paulo Mendes da Rocha, an intervention that significantly modified the original solutions of the project. The kitchen was removed from the interior of the house and was installed on the external patio, in a volume of white painted concrete, under the upper floor slab. A metal gate was placed on the border between the sidewalk and the patio. Cement floors replaced the asphalt floors and the upper part of the circular metal staircase was removed.

James King House
Built in 1972, the King house is located in a gated residential condominium, in the southern region of São Paulo, where large houses of diverse architectural styles coexist with an intense wooded area. The lots of this condominium have approximately two thousand square meters, almost configured as small farms.

The dimensions of the lot and the nature of its surroundings allowed the architect to design the house as an isolated element in the landscape, where the limits of the property can hardly be noticed. The house was built on a single floor with a square plan: a volume of exposed concrete suspended on the ground, supported by pillars over a basement. An opening in this suspended volume creates an illuminated and opened central patio that organizes all the common areas of the house, such as the living room, kitchen, laundry and verandas. The dormitories are lined up on the sunny side of the volume, protected by *brise-soleils*. The house is accessed through a staircase inside the patio.

Adapted to the natural topography of the terrain, the basement is a large, independent, opened and free esplanade, which is only partially under the house, allowing spaces of leisure to be both shaded and sunny. In this basement, besides the swimming pool

絶妙に統合する効果をもたらす。

　洗濯室とエントランス用ベランダを結ぶ廊下は主要ヴォリュームの構成に一役買っている一方で，寝室間の内部動線と併せて建物全体の内回りをなぞるユニークな共用廊下を形成している。

　このような空間構成は住宅内にパーソナルな空間を通る共用動線の重なりを生み，個室のプライベートな性質を覆す。中央のヴォイドを縁取る各スペースの配置と内部動線の組み合わせが居住内の活動を明示し，住宅自体の機能を露わにすることで，外部のランドスケープと対照をなした内部ランドスケープをつくり上げるのだ。

1960年代：危機下に学ぶ
ブラジルの1960年代以降，特に1964年のクーデターとその後の軍事独裁政権の時代は，この国が今日直面している政治的，社会的諸問題を理解するにあたり重要な意味合いを持っている。その時期，世界は冷戦が招いた二極化の重大性に苦しめられていた。合衆国の影響を非常に受けやすいラテン・アメリカ諸国ではこの二極化による複雑な状況変化が軍事独裁政権の確立を促したのだ。

　60年代初め，ブラジリアの落成に加え美術，音楽の分野におけるアヴァンギャルド運動がブラジルに与えたインパクトは楽観的な性質を持つもので，それはまた直近の好調な経済成長や，1958年と1962年のサッカー・ワールドカップでのブラジ

ル勢の栄光にも後押しされていた。こうした出来事が極端な格差社会の深いところに社会的，政治的変化を育む条件を整えたのだ。そして来るべき転換へのシナリオが政情不安を招き，変化への期待の反動として軍事クーデターをもたらした。

　ブラジルにおける21年間にわたる独裁政権時代のうち，1968年から1974年までの期間は抑圧と暴力が最も熾烈だった時期だった。政治的迫害と人権侵害が常態化し，知識層，学生，大学教員らが標的となり日常的に攻撃され投獄や拷問の対象になったのだ。

　1960年代初頭，サンパウロ大学では当時の政治状況を受けて大規模な再構築が行われていた。建築学科においてこの運動を率いていたのは，教授であり建築家のジョアン・バティスタ・ヴィラノヴァ・アルチガス。その頃ヴィラノヴァ・アルチガスは，仕事との関連性そして何より大学と共産党での政治活動が認められ，信望が厚く高い評価を得ており，建築学科の新校舎の設計を任されるほどだった。

　パウロ・メンデス・ダ・ローシャは若き著名建築家として1961年よりヴィラノヴァ・アルチガスに招かれ建築学科の教授を務めていた。二人は当時，教壇に立つ傍ら大学の様々な政治的決定の場面で学生と教員の代表としての役割も果たしており，互いのイデオロギーが歩み寄った瞬間だった。

　1964年にクーデターが勃発，迫害を受け始めたヴィラノヴァ・アルチガスはウルグアイに亡命。1965年にようやくブラジルに帰国，大学に戻り再び教鞭を執り建築学科の校舎建設の指揮をとった。その間メンデス・ダ・ローシャはブラジルに残

on the ground level, there are also the dormitories of employees in an underground level.

The living room is a large space that occupies the central portion of the house, with windows that open towards the patio, and from where it is possible to access the bedrooms. The dormitories are rooms separated by shared bathrooms. The circulation through the dormitories along the sunny side of the volume creates a curious integration between the intimate spaces of the house.

A walkway placed between the laundry area space and the veranda of access, is responsible for composing the main volume and, together with the internal circulation of the dormitories, create a unique common path along the entire perimeter of the house.

This organization of spaces in the house creates an overlap of common circulations through the spaces of individual use and subverts the private aspect of the intimate areas. The organization of spaces around the void associated with this perimeter circulation evidences the internal movements and reveals the functioning of the house itself, creating an internal landscape in contrast to the external landscape.

1960s: Learning years during the crisis
The period beginning in the 1960s in Brazil with the coup in 1964 and its consequent military dictatorship must be seen as an important moment for understanding the political and social problems that the country faces today. During this period, the world was suffering the consequences of polarization of the Cold War. In Latin America, a territory very susceptible to the influence of the United States, the complex developments of this polarization influenced the establishment of military dictatorships.

In Brazil, the 60's began under the impact of the inauguration of Brasilia and avant-garde movements in the field of arts and music. The optimistic characteristic of those years was also a result of the strong economic growth of previous years and the success of the Brazilian football team in the world cups of 1958 and 1962. These events had created the conditions to engender deeper social and political transformations in an extremely unequal society. This scenario of imminent transformation created the political instability that culminated in the military coup, a reaction movement against the aspirations for change.

Within 21 years of dictatorship in Brazil, the period from 1968 to about 1974 were the hardest years of repression and violence, when political persecution and civil rights violations became a common practice. Intellectuals, students and university professors were the targets of constant violations, being subjected to prisons and torture.

In the early 1960's, at the University of São Paulo, the courses underwent profound restructuring inspired by the political environment of the period. In the School of Architecture this movement was led by the professor and architect João Batista Vilanova Artigas. At that moment, Vilanova Artigas enjoyed great prestige and recognition due to the relevance of his work and above all for his political activities in the University and in the Communist Party. His popularity earned him the task of designing the new

り大学での活動，教職に注力した。

1968年12月より政権反対派に対する圧力が益々強くなる。サンパウロ大学は抵抗勢力の牙城であった。建築学科で迫害の的となったのは闘争的な共産主義者であるヴィラノヴァ・アルチガスだった。

1969年2月，政治的緊張の高まりの中，大学の新学期に合わせて建築学科の新校舎ヴィラノヴァ・アルチガス館が落成。この打放しコンクリートの建物ではゆったりとした動線や緩やかなスロープを人々が自由に行き来できるようになっている。プログラムは1枚の光天井に覆われた広い中央ヴォイドの周りに展開され，この空間が建物に公共の広場のような性質と象徴性を付与している。60年代の初めに設計されるも1969年にようやく完成を迎えたこの建物はヴィラノヴァ・アルチガスの最も代表的な作品であり，当時の転換への政治的野心と密接に関わっているものだ。

その数週間後，1969年3月に大阪万国博覧会ブラジル館の設計コンペが開催。万博でブラジルを代表するパヴィリオンの設計はパウロ・メンデス・ダ・ローシャのチームが勝ち取った。メインの広場を覆う薄いコンクリート構造が波打つ基壇で支えられる。ヴィラノヴァ・アルチガスが建築学科校舎のために設計した，1枚の光天井と同じストラクチュアが採用された。

同年4月，政権反対派や左翼系の教授たちが大学から強制的に退職追放されてしまう。その中にはジョアン・バティスタ・ヴィラノヴァ・アルチガス，パウロ・メンデ

ス・ダ・ローシャ，ジョン・メートルジャンが含まれていた。彼らがようやく復帰できたのは1980年のことであった。

以上のような政治上，大学教育上の危機的状況の中で産声を上げたのが，「ミラン邸」と「キング邸」なのである。その意味で，メンデス・ダ・ローシャが大阪万博ブラジル館を通してヴィラノヴァ・アルチガス館に言及するという行為は，彼自身の立ち位置の表明，政治的傾倒の宣言として解釈されるべきだろう。またそれは「ミラン邸」と「キング邸」というプロジェクト，特にそのプログラムの構成を解く鍵ともなるはずである。

*元はフェルナンド・ミランのために設計されたものであるが，2000年代の初めにエドゥアルド・レミが買受け，パウロ・メンデス・ダ・ローシャの指揮の下，リノベーションが施された。

（和訳：谷理佐）

building of the School of Architecture.

Paulo Mendes da Rocha was a distinguished young architect who, since 1961, by invitation of Vilanova Artigas, was a professor at the School of Architecture. In those years, besides the teaching practice, the two architects acted as representatives of students and professors in many political and decisive instances of the University. This period was the moment of ideological approach between these architects.

With the coup of 1964, Vilanova Artigas began to be persecuted and therefore went to exile in Uruguay, returning to Brazil only in 1965, when he took up the teaching practice and the coordination of the construction of the building of the School of Architecture. Meanwhile, Mendes da Rocha stayed in Brazil, dedicated to his office and classes at the University.

From December 1968 the government started increasing the pressure against the opposition to the regime. The University of São Paulo was a stronghold of resistance. In the School of Architecture, the focus of the persecutions was the communist militant Vilanova Artigas.

In February of 1969, alongside the increase of political tension, the building of the School of Architecture was inaugurated at the beginning of the school year. Built in exposed concrete, the Vilanova Artigas school is a building where users can freely ramble along gentle ramps and generous circulations. The program is organized around a large central void covered by a single illuminated ceiling, a space that adds to the building the qualities and symbologies of a public square. Designed at the beginning of the

decade but only completed in 69, this building, very representative of the work of Vilanova Artigas, was closely related to the transformative political aspirations of that period.

In the following weeks, in March 1969, an architecture competition for the Brazilian Pavilion at the Expo '70 in Osaka was held. The pavilion that was chosen to represent Brazil at the Expo, won by the team led by Paulo Mendes da Rocha, was composed by a thin concrete structure protecting the pavilion's main square which was supported by a rippled floor. The structure was the same single illuminated ceiling designed by Vilanova Artigas for the Architecture School building.

In April of that same year, several professors of the University, opposed to the regime or affiliated to the left wing, were expelled from the University, being compulsorily retired. Among them were João Batista Vilanova Artigas, Paulo Mendes da Rocha and Jon Maitrejean. These professors would only be reintegrated in 1980.

It was in this context of crisis associated to political and professional learning that the Millan and King houses were conceived. In this sense, the gesture of mentioning Vilanova Artigas building in the Brazilian Pavilion should be understood as a positioning statement, a declaration of his political affiliation that also explains the projects of Millan and King houses, especially in the way the issues related to the organization of the programs were solved.

*In the early 2000s the house originally designed for Fernando Millan was bought by Eduardo Leme, who did a renovation under the coordination of Paulo Mendes da Rocha.

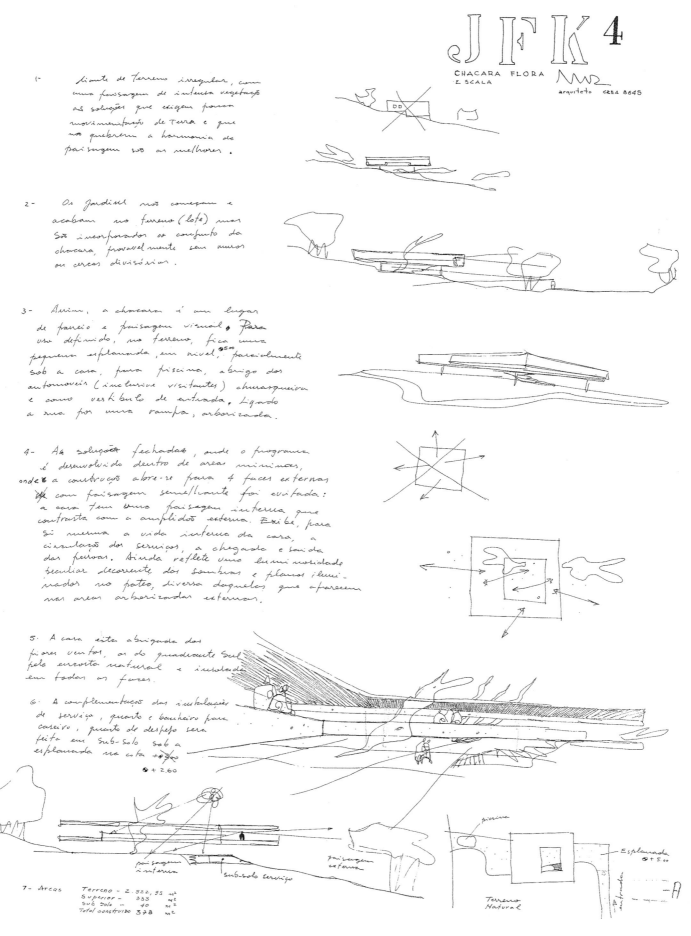

Sketch by Paulo Mendes da Rocha

King House 1972

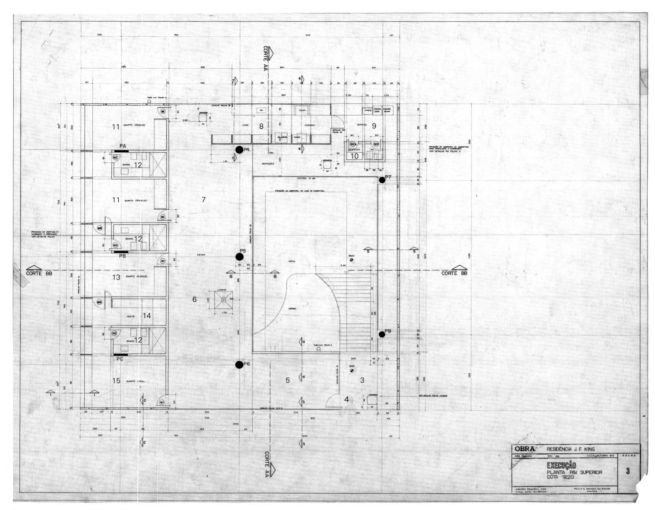

First floor (level 92.20)

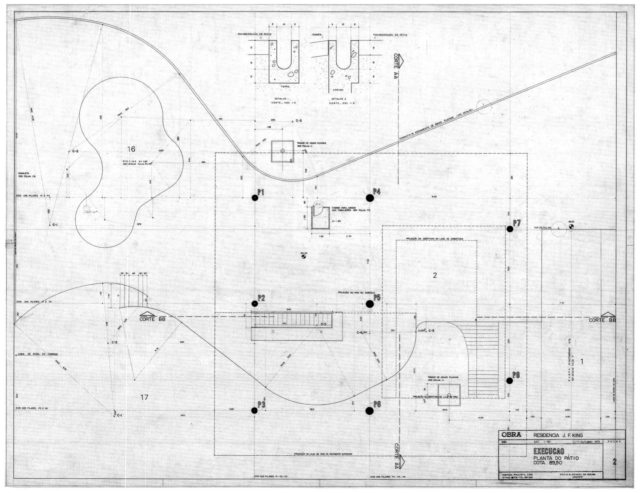

Ground floor (level 89.50)   S=1:250

1	APPROACH
2	PATIO
3	ENTRANCE PORCH
4	ENTRANCE
5	STUDY/LOUNGE
6	LIVING ROOM
7	DINING ROOM
8	KITCHEN
9	SERVICE
10	PANTRY
11	CHILDREN'S ROOM
12	BATHROOM
13	GUEST ROOM
14	CLOSET
15	MASTER BEDROOM
16	POOL
17	GARDEN

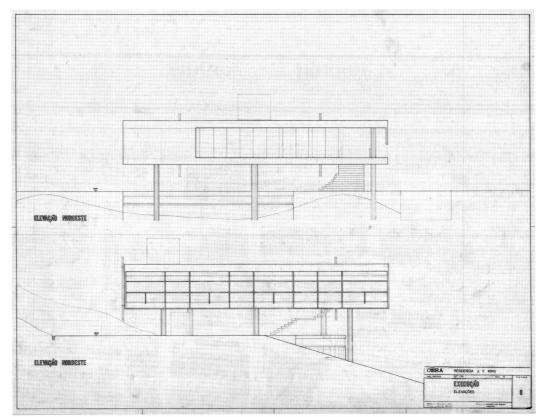

Northwest elevation (above), northeast elevation (below) S=1:300

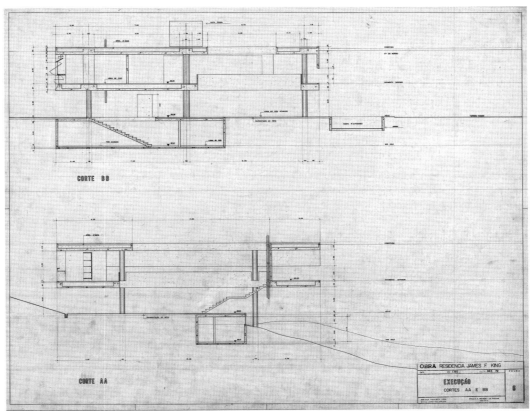

Sections S=1:300

(p.10: caption of sketches)
1. Due to the irregular topography, of dense greenery landscape, the best solution is to avoid soil movement, not to break the landscape harmony.

2. The gardens do not begin nor end in the lot. Instead, are incorporated to the farm, probably with no walls or border fences.

3. Therefore, the farm is a place where to walk around and enjoy the landscape. There is a small esplanade on level +5.00, partially underneath the house, for specific purpose: the swimming pool, a parking lot (also for visitors), a barbecue place, and an entrance hall connected to the street by a ramp.

4. Closed solutions were avoided where the program is developed in minimal areas, where the construction opens itself towards the four external faces with similar landscape view: the house has an internal landscape that contrasts with the external amplitude. It shows, for itself, the internal life of the house, the circulation of service areas, the entrance and exit of people. It also has a peculiar luminosity, caused by shadows and illuminated planes on the patio, different from the one that is seen on the external greenery.

5. The house is sheltered from the most severe winds, those coming from the south quadrant, by the natural and sunny slopes in all faces.

6. The installation of services, bedroom and bathroom for housekeeper, deposit, is complemented underground, under the esplanade, at +2.60 level.

7. Areas
Lot: 2,522.95 m² / Upper floor: 333.00 m² / Basement: 40.00 m² /
Total constructed area: 373.00 m²

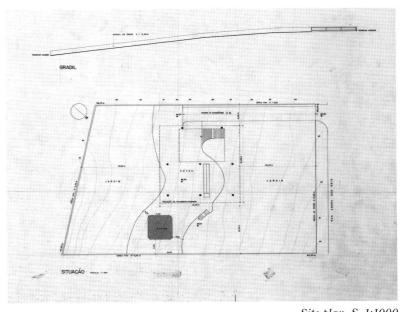

Site plan S=1:1000

Southwest elevation: view toward west corner

Southwest elevation: one of columns supporting whole building on center. View toward patio

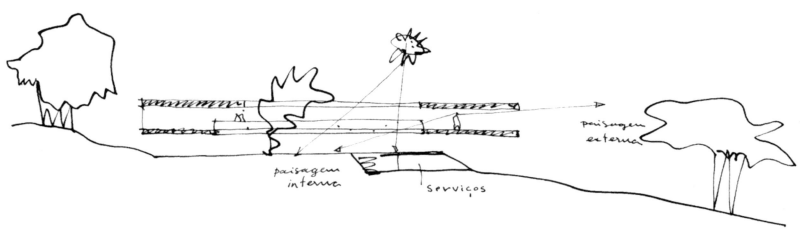

paisagem
interna

serviços

paisagem
externa

Sketch by Paulo Mendes da Rocha

Looking toward patio from approach. Pool inmost

View from garden on north

Northeast elevation covered with brise-soleil

View over pool from east

Patio: looking southwest. Staircase leads to caretaker's room on basement

View toward patio from northwest. Caretaker's room below

Patio: view toward grand stairs to first floor

Spandrel walls facing patio are painted cyan. View toward pool

◁ *Grand stairs to first floor*

Corridor connecting rooms. Inside of hanging wall is painted magenta

Entrance porch at landing of stair. Glazed entrance on right

Looking northeast from entrance porch

Study and lounge: view from entrance. Built-in table leg has similar figure with column

Corner of living room: curved spandrel wall acts as balcony when glazed doors are opened

Glazed doors are opened

Living room. Study/lounge on right

Fireplace at living room

Detail of windows of living room facing patio

Dining room. View toward living room

East corner with planting. Kitchen behind wall

Looking through living/dining room from south. Windows open

Corridor along northeast. Children's rooms line up on left. Holizontal slab installed along window serves as desk

Bathroom with toplight

Detail of brise-soleil

Kitchen on southeast side

Perspective of building surrounding patio

View from street on south

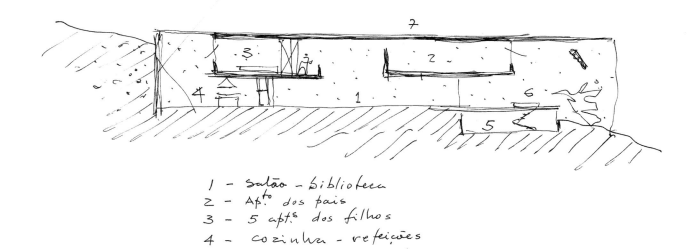

1 - Salão - biblioteca
2 - Apt.º dos pais
3 - 5 apt.s dos filhos
4 - cozinha - refeições
5 - serviço
6 - Pateo de entrada
7 - Teto jardim

casa Millan

Sketch by Paulo Mendes da Rocha

1	PATIO	8	BATHROOM
2	ENTRANCE	9	BEDROOM
3	LIVING ROOM	10	POOL
4	LIBRARY	11	GARDEN
5	LUNCH ROOM	12	LAUNDRY
6	KITCHEN	13	CARETAKER'S ROOM
7	STUDIO	14	STORAGE

Basement

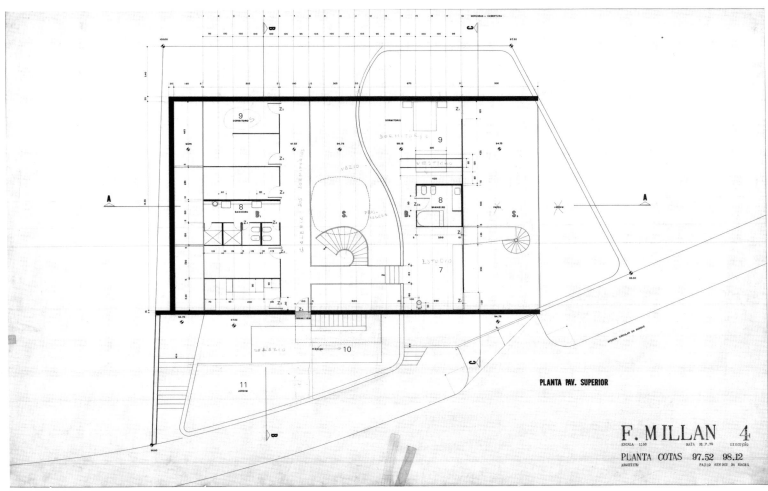

First floor

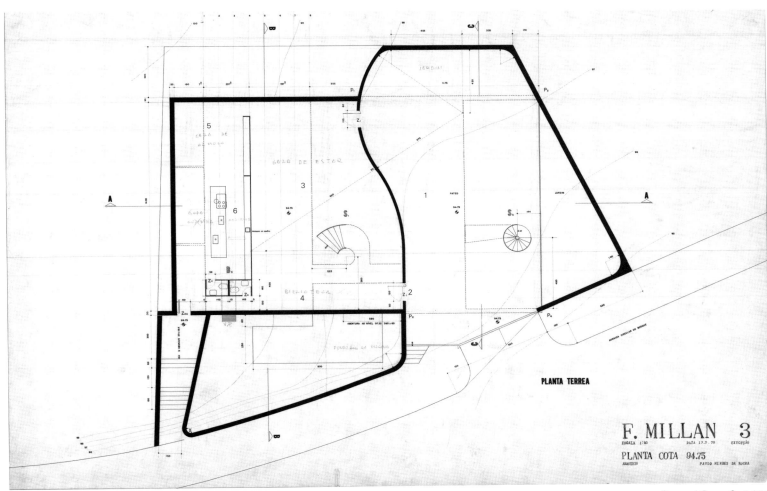

Ground floor S=1:250

Entrance patio. Spiral stair leads to basement

View toward garden on basement

Entrance

Living room with characteristic S-shaped wall and toplight. Winding staircase on right

Living room in dougle-height. Entrance on left inmost

Details of staircase △▽

Living room: looking west

Downward view of staircase

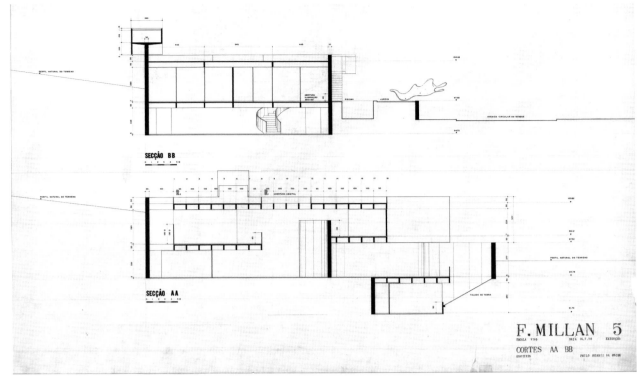

Section AA (below), section BB (above) S=1:300

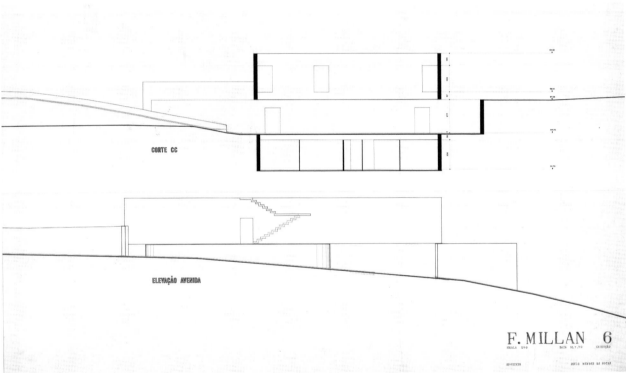

Section CC (above), south elevation (below)

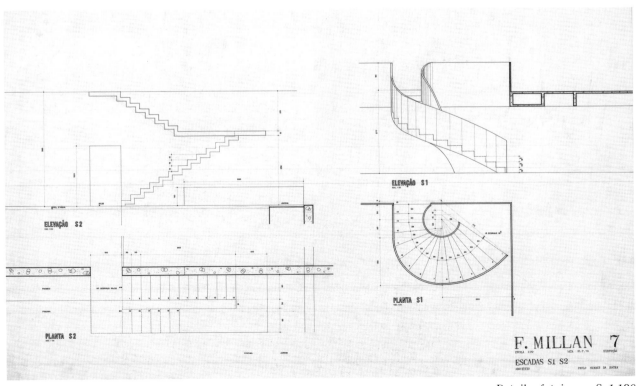

Details of staircase S=1:120

Dining room

Gallery (originally kitchen) with linear toplight

Gallery (originally kitchen) with double-height void

View from first floor. S-shaped spandrel wall

View from landing of staircase

Connecting corridor. View toward studio. Entrance on right below

Looking south from corridor on first floor. Bedrooms on right

Master bedroom

Master bathroom

Window detail

Bathroom

Terrace and pool on street side of first floor. View of exterior stairs to roof terrace

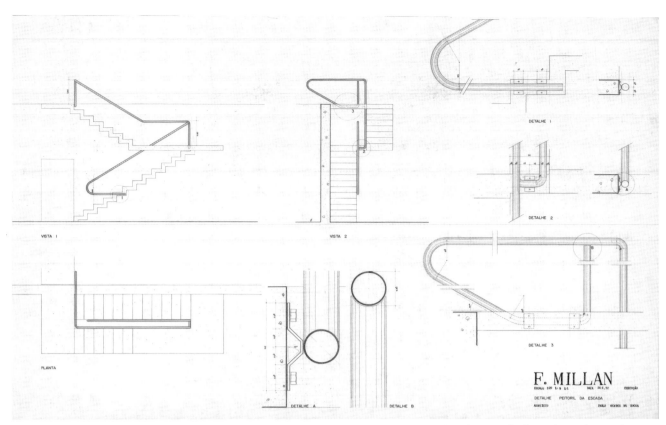

Details of handrail of exterior staircase S=1:120

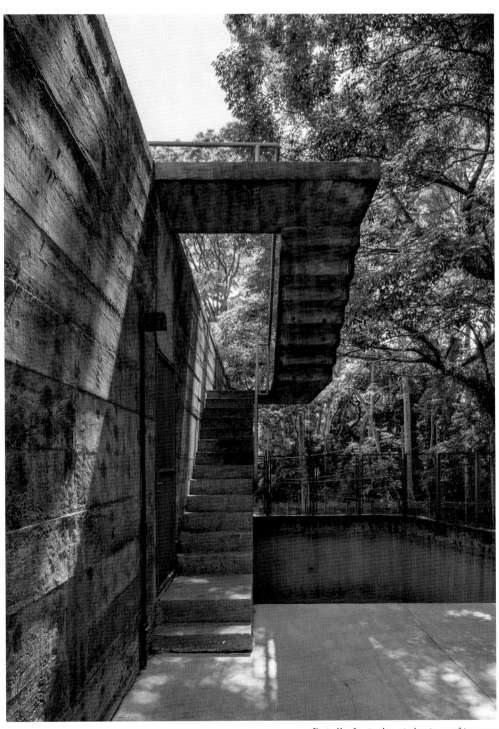

Detail of exterior stairs to roof terrace

Roof terrace with water court

世界現代住宅全集 27
パウロ・メンデス・ダ・ローシャ
キング邸
ミラン／レミ邸
2018 年 5 月 24 日発行
文：ジョゼ・パウロ・ゴヴェア
撮影・編集：二川由夫
アート・ディレクション：細谷巖

印刷・製本：大日本印刷株式会社
制作・発行：エーディーエー・エディタ・トーキョー
151-0051　東京都渋谷区千駄ヶ谷 3-12-14
TEL.（03）3403-1581（代）

ISBN 978-4-87140-560-7 C1352